DEEP SEA DISCOVERIES

Simon Chapman

Badger Publishing Limited
Oldmedow Road,
Hardwick Industrial Estate,
King's Lynn PE30 4JJ
Telephone: 01553 816083

www.badgerlearning.co.uk

2 4 6 8 10 9 7 5 3 1

Deep Sea Discoveries ISBN 978-1-78837-571-9

Text © Simon Chapman

Complete work © Badger Publishing Limited 2022

All rights reserved. No part of this publication may be reproduced, stored in any form or by any means mechanical, electronic, recording or otherwise without the prior permission of the publisher.

The right of Simon Chapman to be identified as author of this work has been asserted by them in accordance with the Copyright, Designs and Patents Act 1988.

Commissioning Editor: Sarah Rudd
Copyeditor: Carrie Lewis
Designer: Adam Wilmott

Cover Image: Shutterstock/superjoseph
Page 4: Juliet Breese
Page 5: Juliet Breese
Page 6: Juliet Breese
Page 7: Shutterstock/Kondratuk Aleksei, SPL/DANTE FENOLIO
Page 9: Shutterstock/Kondratuk Aleksei
Page 10: Alamy/BIOSPHOTO
Page 11: Alamy/Adisha Pramod, SPL/DANTE FENOLIO
Page 12: Shutterstock/Sabelskaya
Page 13: Shutterstock/Dotted Yeti
Page 14: Shutterstock/Solodov Aleksei and Shutterstock/klyaksun
Page 15: Ocean Exploration Trust/NautilusLive
Page 16: Ocean Exploration Trust/NautilusLive
Page 17: Ocean Exploration Trust/NautilusLive
Page 18: Alamy/Adisha Pramod
Page 19: Ocean Exploration Trust/NautilusLive, SPL/PHILIPPE CRASSOUS
Page 20: Allan C. Green 1878 - 1954 via Wikimedia Commons
Page 21: Office of Naval Research via Wikimedia Commons
Page 22: Richard Varcoe on behalf of Caladan Oceanic LLC via Wikimedia Commons
Page 23: Alamy/Everett Collection Inc
Page 24: Naval History & Heritage Command via Wikimedia Commons
Page 25: Shutterstock/Andriy Nekrasov
Page 26: Shutterstock/Galeshnikov Aleksandr
Page 27: Shutterstock/Mr Dasenna
Page 28: Ocean Exploration Trust/NautilusLive
Page 29: Shutterstock/Antonov Maxim

Every effort has been made to contact copyright holders of material reproduced in this book. Any omissions will be rectified in subsequent printings if notice is given to the publisher.

DEEP SEA DISCOVERIES

Contents

1. Sinking, Sinking, Sinking!	4
2. Creatures of the Deep	9
3. The Ooze: Mud with Attitude	14
4. Deep Ocean Exploration	20
5. Deep Sea Shipwrecks	23
6. Saving the Sea Bed	25
Glossary	30
Questions	31
Index	32

Badger
LEARNING

1. Sinking, Sinking, Sinking!

You are in a unique submarine that can dive all the way to the ocean floor. It is called a Deep Submergence Vehicle, known as a DSV.

Words highlighted in this colour are in the glossary on page 30

The water around you darkens through blue into black as you submerge deeper and deeper. 200 metres. 300 metres. No light reaches down here. All you can see are the readings on your DSV's depth control panel as you continue downwards. 1000 metres. 1100 metres...

The DSV's compartment is a sphere, like a ball. This is the best shape to stop the pressure of the water all around from squashing it. The weak points are at the windows. They are not as strong as the DSV's steel hull.

You are so deep now that any leak would spurt across like a water jet. It would slice through everything inside like a cutting laser, including you!

You can't see or feel that you are descending deeper into the water as everything is so dark outside. You could be in outer space. It would be just as black and you would be just as alone. You listen out for creaks in the DSV's metal shell. You hear no noise apart from the whirring of the engine and your own breathing.

Instrument checks. Temperature four degrees Celsius. Just above freezing. The temperature has stayed roughly the same since 1000 metres.

You look at your instrument panel. Your **sonar** sends out high-pitched sound waves which echo back from the seabed to tell you how far away it is. Nothing shows on your monitor screen. There is no chance of hitting anything for two or three kilometres yet.

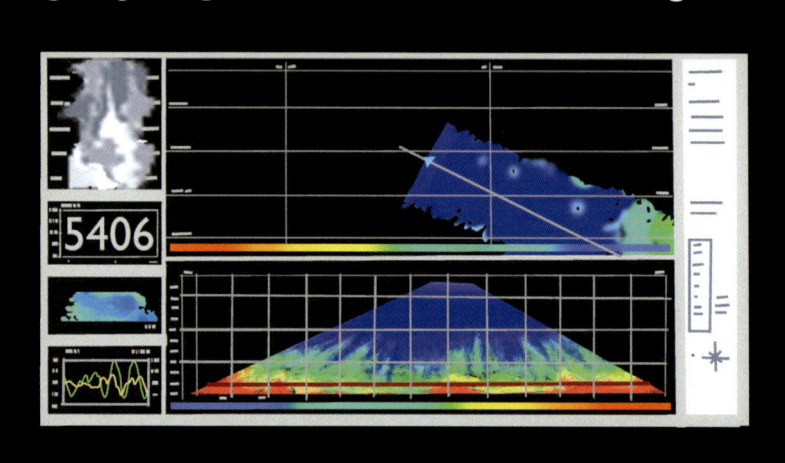

A light flashes outside. Your eyes pick up rows of green and blue lights pulsing upwards in waves. A jellyfish; this one is called a comb jelly. It is the size and shape of a jam jar. Its body is transparent, with tiny hairs along the sides which ripple to transport it through the sea. Tentacles underneath its body extend out and pick up specks of food in the water.

Another light. Yellow this time. The yellow light is fixed on a stalk, which is protruding from a fish's head above its mouth. This is an anglerfish. The fishing rod light is to attract other creatures, so the anglerfish can snap them up.

The comb jelly and the anglerfish slowly disappear from view as you adjust the DSV's controls and carry on downwards.

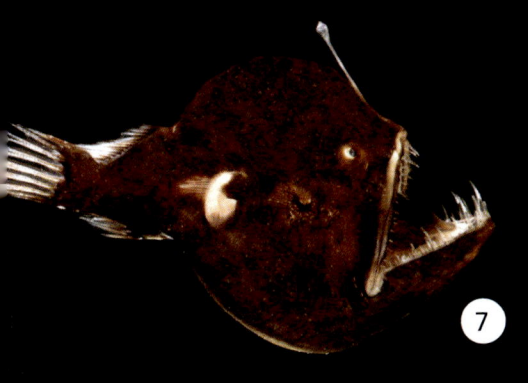

Total blackness. It's an alien world out there, less understood than outer space, but much closer. Just two kilometres above is daylight, wind, clouds, fresh air to breathe, all in a space with a safe, and pressure that won't crush you.

But right now, you're here in the ocean depths, a place that takes up 95 per cent of the living space on our planet, but will kill you in an instant if anything goes wrong.

Scientific Name	Nickname	Depth
Epipelagic Zone	The Sunlight Zone	Up to 200m
Mesopelagic Zone	The Twilight Zone	200–1000m
Bathypelagic Zone	The Midnight Zone	1000–4000m
Abyssopelagic Zone	The Abyss	4000–6000m
Hadalpelagic Zone	The Trenches	6000–11000m

WOW! facts

The Earth's oceans are so deep that they contain whole unseen mountain ranges that are even bigger than the Himalayas.

2. Creatures of the Deep

Seventy-nine per cent of planet Earth's **biosphere**, the space where living things exist, lies more than 1000 metres down in the oceans. With no sunlight, there are no plants. So, what does everything eat? The answer is 'marine snow'. This is the name for the pieces of dead plants and animal matter that drifts down from the zones above.

Most of the sea animals in the ocean depths give out light, known as bioluminescence. The light is usually green or blue as these colours travel best through water. Some shrimps are coloured red which makes them almost invisible, as red light is absorbed by sea water.

Salps

Salps are like tiny tubes that suck sea water through their bodies and feed on **organisms**. There can be millions swimming around together.

Siphonophores

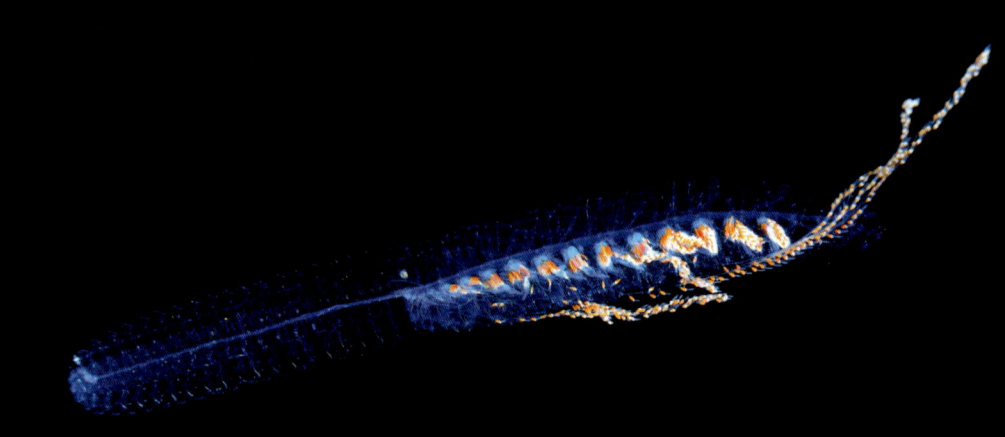

Siphonophores are colonies of sea creatures and when they join together can be over 40 metres long, which is longer than a blue whale, the world's largest animal. However, the width of the colony is tiny at around two centimetres, roughly the same width as a broom handle.

Each creature carries out a different job and they rely on each other for survival. Some have stinging cells whilst some attract and catch prey. Other creatures squirt water through their bodies to move the siphonophore along.

Fish

Lanternfish are easily the most common fish in the deep oceans. They are a few centimetres long and have lights along their sides and bellies. Scientists think that the lights disguise them from predators. Every night, huge shoals of lanternfish move to the ocean's surface where there is more food to eat.

Gulper eels are actually stange-looking fish who have enormous mouths that stretch to fit in any fish or squid they can find in the blackness. They have extremely long tails that help them move through the water, which are so long they can sometimes become knotted.

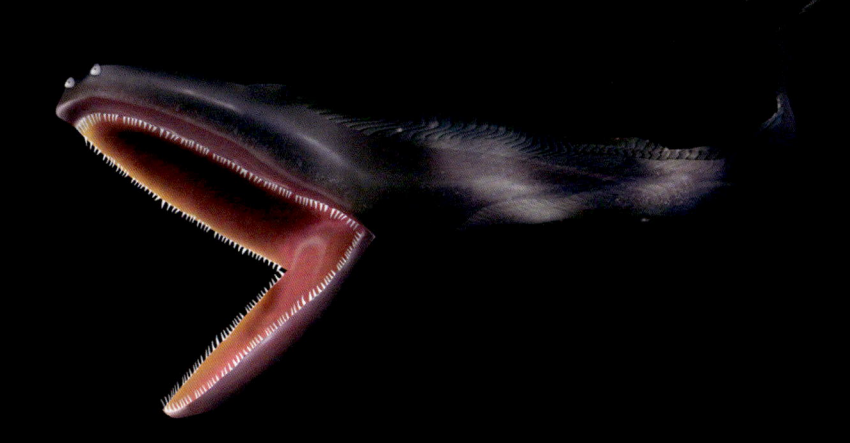

Giant squid

For centuries, stories of giant squid have been told in cultures all around the world. Squid with tentacles 15 metres long, which is longer than bus, have washed up on beaches. Sperm whales have even been found with sucker marks across their bodies.

Scientists are now using DSV's with special sensors to find giant squid in the blackness and underwater cameras to film them.

Characteristics of a giant squid include:
- eyes that are up to 25 centimetres across – the biggest eyes in the animal kingdom
- a sharp beak
- eight arms to grab prey
- long tentacles tipped with saw-edged suckers.

Greenland shark

The Greenland shark is a fascinating creature which mainly lives in the Arctic ocean. They are very rarely seen because they can dive to extreme depths up to 2200 metres.

Other amazing facts about the Greenland shark include:
- Their average lifespan is 390 years with the oldest known shark living to 512! This means there are still likely to be Greenland sharks in the ocean that were alive during the Great Fire of London in 1666.
- They can grow to over six metres and weigh up to 1000 kilograms.
- Their flesh is poisonous due to **toxins** which help them cope with the extreme cold and water pressure.

3. The Ooze: Mud with Attitude!

The ocean floor teems with life like the watery world above it. Mud coats the sea bed and when this mud is full of animal and plant matter, it is called 'ooze'. The ooze swarms with bacteria, worms and shrimp-like creatures called amphipods. They burrow through the slop, feeling for anything they can eat.

Whale falls

The ooze is especially full of life where a dead whale lies on the sea bed because the huge body provides a sudden feast for the creatures that dwell here.

First to arrive are fast-moving **scavengers**, like hagfish and sleeper sharks, that bite off chunks of the whale's flesh. Slower moving crabs, squat lobsters and octopi join them.

In the cold waters, whale meat can take three years to rot. The scavengers break the carcass down so that only its skeleton is left – and then that is eaten by bone-eating worms.

Bone-eating worms live off the bacteria that feed on the whale carcass. They do not have mouth parts or stomachs and scientists still don't understand how they digest their food to stay alive.

Mussels, clams and sea snails feed on the bacteria too. They finish eating every last piece of the dead whale in 50 to 100 years. All that is left behind is ooze.

WOW! facts

Hagfish have fixed mouths which cannot open and close. When a predator attacks, they shoot a sticky slime which can glue up their attacker's mouth.

Hydrothermal vents

Hydrothermal vents are extremely hot springs at the bottom of the ocean. They form along ocean ridges about 2500 metres down, where the continents pull apart.

Seawater within cracks in the ocean bed is heated to hundreds of degrees Celsius by the Earth's underlying mantle. This water spurts out of vents in the ocean bed, which contains minerals, as well as hydrogen sulphide, a gas which stinks like rotten eggs!

As the hot water touches the cooler sea water around it, the minerals become solid and build up into chimney stacks, which can end up taller than houses.

Living the hot life

Bacteria live on the chimney stacks and, in turn, crabs, shrimp and worms feed on the bacteria.

All these animals survive without the need for sunlight. Some scientists think this is how life originally started on Earth. Others say if there is life on other planets, it could be similar to this.

In the extreme pressure and total blackness, most creatures do not have eyes as there is no need for them, and instead use their sense of touch to feel their way around.

Yeti crabs have claws are covered in spines to trap and farm bacteria they will later eat. The spines are also thought to remove the poison from the bacteria.

A magnified image of a deep ocean worm.

Deep ocean worms can be found on live and extinct hydrothermal vents. Many of them have spiny growths along their heads and bodies, which make them look very alien!

Giant tube worms can be up to a metre long and have no digestive system. Instead, their nutrients are provided by bacteria that live inside them. They take in oxygen from the water through a bright red fan of blood vessels, which they pull in very quickly if anything threatening comes near them.

4. Deep Ocean Exploration

The deepest point on Earth's surface is Challenger Deep in the Marianas Trench. It was named after the ship HMS *Challenger*, which made the first survey of the ocean depths between 1872 and 1876.

HMS *Challenger* was a sailing ship but it also had a steam engine for when there was no wind. Its crew dropped very long ropes to measure how deep the ocean was and dragged nets across the seabed to find out what was living there.

When they pulled up the creatures from the ocean floor, the change in pressure had caused them to explode!

Expeditions

Many journeys have been made into the deep sea to try and uncover more information about the least known area on planet Earth. Even today, we have better maps of Mars than we do of the ocean floor.

Bathysphere 1934: This was the first deep sea vessel used to observe marine life in its natural habitat. It was lowered on a cable over the side of a ship and reached a depth of 923 metres.

DSV *Alvin* 1964: *Alvin* has completed over 5000 expeditions, including the Marianas Trench. In 1986, *Alvin* explored the wreck of the steamship, Titanic.

WOW! facts

Alvin was once attacked by a swordfish 600 metres down off the coast of Florida, USA. The fish's 'sword' got stuck in the side of the submarine. *Alvin*'s crew had to surface with the swordfish still attached. They cooked the fish and ate it!

Deepsea Challenger 2012: Hollywood film producer James Cameron, who made films such as *Titanic* and *The Abyss*, wanted to explore, the bottom of Challenger Deep. His journey to the deepest point in the Marianas Trench took two hours 37 minutes. The pilot's area of this DSV was tiny and only had room for one person.

Triton DSV *Limiting Factor* 2017: This vehicle was used in the Five Deeps Expedition, a mission to visit the deepest point in each of the Earth's five oceans. It broke the world record for the deepest crewed descent at 10,925 metres. In total, the expedition covered 87,000 kilometres in 10 months, over a total of 39 dives, and discovered 40 new deep sea creatures.

WOW! facts
The crew of DSV *Alvin* tied polystyrene cups to the outside of the vessel just to see what would happen. The pressure squashed the cups to the size of thimbles.

5. Deep Sea Shipwrecks

How do you explore a shipwreck when it is sitting on the ocean bed several kilometres underwater?

Titanic

The wreck of *Titanic* is the most famous shipwreck of all time. People have wondered where exactly the wreck lay on the ocean bed since it sank in 1912.

When it was finally discovered in 1986, the team who explored the wreck used DSV *Alvin* and a remotely controlled vehicle connected by a cable.

This was the first time anyone had seen the *Titanic* in 75 years. The wreck was extremely rusty, with huge parts of it missing, but the grand staircase could still be recognised.

USS Johnston

The deepest known shipwreck in the world is the destroyer USS *Johnston*, which sank in the Pacific Ocean in 1944 during World War II. The wreck lies, half covered in mud, at a depth of 6500 metres.

In 2021, a **salvage** crew filmed the wreck with an remotely controlled vehicle. Two people have since gone down in DSV *Limiting Factor* to have a closer look. They found the ship mainly intact with its guns still facing in the direction they were firing.

6. Saving the Sea Bed

Although we do not know much about the deepest waters on Earth, it is clear that humans are having an impact on them.

Plastic crisis

In 2021, a new type of shrimp was discovered inside the ooze, seven kilometres down in the Marianas Trench.

The scientists who discovered the shrimp were excited by their discovery. However, they were shocked by what they found inside its gut – tiny pieces of plastic.

Somehow our waste had made it all the way down into the most unknown **ecosystem** on the planet.

WOW! facts

Every year, eight million tonnes of plastic end up in the world's oceans. That's the same as dumping a lorry load of plastic in the sea every minute of the year. Overall, there are estimated to be 5.25 trillion pieces of plastic currently in our oceans.

Ocean dumping
Unfortunately, the ocean floor is often used as a dumping ground for all sorts of waste, including nuclear and industrial waste. This heavily effects marine life.

Fifty years ago, 387,000 tonnes of pharmaceutical waste was dumped into the deep sea off the coast of Puerto Rico. Thousands of barrels, weighing the same as 880 jumbo jets, leaked into the sea.

There are now rules on what can and cannot be dumped in the ocean. However, not everyone listens to the rules and companies still dump hazardous waste illegally into the ocean to this day.

'The ocean is not a dumping ground. It is quite likely where life originated from. While we can forgive previous generations for not fully recognizing the importance of a clean ocean for life on this planet, there is no excuse today. The science and knowledge about how important the ocean is to the existence of life — ours included — is now widely understood.'

Sylvia Earle, ocean explorer

Deep-sea mining

In places, the ocean floor mud contains potato-sized chunks of rare metals, like manganese and cobalt. These metals are needed to make batteries for electric cars.

Mining companies want to bring the metals to the surface but some people believe that the deep sea should be left alone.

The mud which coats the ocean bed is important to the planet's climate as it stores carbon. Mining would release this carbon and make climate change worse.

The deep sea is like an alien world because of its extreme conditions, such as complete darkness, crushing pressure and cold temperature.

As humans, we will never be able to experience anything like it, but this does not mean we have the right to damage it. We need to look after the deep sea or face the extinction of many species, including ourselves.

7 Ways To Reduce Ocean Pollution

1. Reduce Your Use of Single-Use Plastics
Wherever you live, the easiest and most direct way that you can get started is by buying products we can reuse.

2. Recycle Properly
When you use plastics that can be recycled, always be sure to recycle them. Just 9 per cent of plastic is recycled worldwide.

3. Clean the Beach
Help remove plastics from the ocean and prevent them from getting there in the first place by removing litter from the beach.

4. Support Bans
Many places around the world have banned on single use plastic bags, takeout containers, and bottles. You can support these bans wherever you are.

5. Avoid Microbeads
Tiny plastic particles, called microbeads, have become a growing source of ocean plastic pollution in recent years. Take care not to buy products that contain these.

6. Spread the Word
Keep up to date with issues related to ocean pollution and help make others aware of the problem. Tell your friends and family about how they can be part of the solution.

7. Support Organisations
There are many organisations working to reduce and eliminate ocean pollution. These organisations rely on help from people like you to continue their important work.

GLOSSARY

biosphere — a part of the world where life can exist

ecosystem — a community of organisms and their environment

molten magma — liquid rock underneath Earth's surface

organism — any living thing

pharmaceutical — a medicinal drug

salvage — to save something from harm or rescue

scavenger — an animal that feeds on dead or decaying material

shoal — a group of fish that stay together

sonar — a device used for detecting objects underwater

toxin — any poisonous substance that is produced by living cells or living organisms

Questions

Why does an anglerfish have a light above its head? *(page 7)*

Which creature can have eyes up to 25 centimetres across? *(page 12)*

What do bone-eating worms feed off? *(page 16)*

Why is the deepest ocean trench called Challenger Deep? *(page 20)*

How many expeditions has the SV Alvin completed? *(page 21)*

Name two ways in which we can reduce ocean pollution *(page 29)*

INDEX

abyssopelagic zone 8
amphipod 14
anglerfish 7
Arctic ocean 13
bathypelagic zone 8
bioluminescence 9
biosphere 9
bone-eating worms 15, 16
Challenger Deep 20-22
comb jelly 7
deep ocean worms 19
DSV (Deep Submergence Vehicle) 4-7, 12, 21-24
epipealgic zone 8
giant squid 12
giant tube worms 19
Greenland shark 13
gulper eels 11
hadalpelagic zone 8
hagfish 15, 16
HMS *Challenger* 20
hydrothermal vents 17, 19
lanternfish 11
Marianas Trench 8, 20, 21, 25
marine snow 9
mesopelagic zone 8
mining 28
ocean zones 8
ooze 14-16
Puerto Rico 26
salps 9
siphonophores 10
sonar 6
swordfish 21
Titanic 21-23
USS *Johnston* 24
whale 10, 12, 15, 16
yeti crab 18